Everything In-between

Poetic Musings

By: Jayne Yu

Everything In-Between

Poetic Musings

First paperback edition November 2020

Book design by: AtriTeX

ISBN 9798575758372

Published by Ithiel Publishing

Hi there, thank you for purchasing this book.

Although we are all on different journeys in life, there are some experiences we go through that are somewhat recognizable or relatable. My hope is that you will find those moments on these pages, that there will be a familiarity or a sense of wonder in the words you read and that they would touch you in some way.

"Deep calls unto deep..." Psalm 42:7

-Jayne-

This book is dedicated to my Heavenly Father

Thank you for your unwavering love and for relentlessly reminding me who you created me to be

You are my reason for being.

Contents

Part I

Part II

Part III

Part IV

Part I

Speaking Without Words

It's the look in your eyes that tell the story
It's the look that gives you away
no matter how hard you try
to conceal your emotions
It's the look that speaks for your mouth
when it wants to remain shut
It's the look of absolute transparency
A look of surrender with a fight
A fight already lost

Waiting For You

In the midst of chaos
there is a calmness that sits
waiting to be acknowledged
To be approached
Sometimes it slips our mind
when everything is in turmoil
and our attention
reverts back to ourselves
trying to make sense of nonsense
on our own terms
In search for the grain of truth
that could possibly bring enlightenment
to the lack of understanding we confess
The cycle continues
In the midst of disorder
there is someone
waiting to be recognized
Waiting to provide
Waiting to comfort
Someone
waiting just for you

Free

I want to see what we can't envision with our own eyes
I want to search for something that hasn't been lost
But something that's been forsaken
I want to grasp a hold of something intangible
Something I can never call my own
I want to fly anywhere the wind won't take me
I want to be where no one wants to be
A place where people fear to be
A place called me
A place so carefree
I want to be *me*

Closure

I need time
Time can be our enemy
but in moments it can be our best friend
Perhaps our only friend
I stood in silence
my tongue tied in knots
as my mind took a stroll down memory lane
I felt his heart ache
and the weight of hurt
caused my heart to sink
Everything is a blur
My eyes start to sting
then slowly comes the stream
peacefully trickling down my face
where it stops to rest at the peak of my lip
before it continues it's journey once again
I quickly gather my thoughts
and as I'm about to utter some words
I feel as though I've taken a sip of the ocean
Silence fills the air
the thought of walking away
keeps crossing my mind
Each second feels like an eternity
He's drowned himself in his own senseless tears again
Witnessing this makes me feel suffocated
I don't want to swim in his pool
I struggle to keep our eyes unlocked
gazing in the distance beyond him
Finally I collect myself
My eyes meet his

and I watch as his face begs for another chance
I wonder how quickly I would've disappeared
if it weren't for his tears
Time, it's not what I need
I need closure
and it's time

Tug of War

Trying to control the uncontrollable
feels like a constant battle I'll never win
Afraid of the unknown outcome
of what it's all about
whether it's temporary or permanent
A strict emotion or lenient
Struggling with distinguishing the difference
between a feeling that rests in a moment
or takes residence for the time to come

Childhood

I longed for the warmth
of a love lost
in the most crucial days
of my life
Hardly discovered
Barely visible
A love never fully understood
An affection never known
It was the warmth
I desired to bask in
even when the heat
was too much to bear
I felt too much of the cold
frozen most of my life
It was what I reached for
but could never really touch
I could not understand
why it felt so far and out of reach
I wondered why others swam in it
while I sat waiting on dry cement
hoping that I, too
would be blessed with a pool of my own

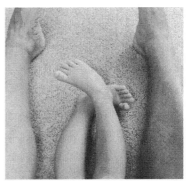

Sunny Days

Every visit
with the greeting of your face
brings great joy
Every departure
that ends with a hug and barely a kiss
leaves me feeling heartbroken
Broken from the years of absence
Years of unforgiveness
bitterness and anger
Feelings that kept me from the truth
of who you are to me
and the meaning of that relationship
I won't look back
I can only regret as I reflect
on the times that could've been

Every visit
I leave in tears
The image of you
engraved in my mind
speaks too loudly of the years I've missed out on
The neglected times
It hurts me so much
but I love you with a tighter grip
Your image is a memory
I don't want to remember
It's an image
I wish I could recreate

Denial

I cry the tears
you never allowed to fall
I feel the pain
you hid so well
So deep inside
you let it build a place of its own
Now I can see
how it's affected you
I watch in silence
as you speak without a sound
The choices you made
were for your own good
However, I cannot help
but feel there's so much more
to what you pretend
is long out the door
Every now and then
you play it cool
when I know all that within you
wants to let go
and free itself
from all the layers it hides beneath
Your life has been
anything but a fairytale
You ran so fast
from the place that frightened you
Trying to outrun yourself
from the love that lingered
Just waiting for you to take it
Instead, you hid under

any wing that covered you
and stayed until it flew away
leaving you alone once again

The Moment

One moment
can linger
longer than intended
But the feeling
in that moment
can never be expressed
in the way it was felt
at the time
The moment
unforgettable
unchangeable
unattainable
One moment
that will remain
A moment
to remember

Possibilities

I'm waiting
for the stars to fall
one by two
I wait
only to be welcomed
by a silence
that stings my heart
I'm on the receiving end
of a delay
and I cannot manage
the consequences
It's a relentless conflict
battling within
which erupts in silence
The reaction
so permanent
yet fleeting
A feeling so rare
It must be captured
in its full essence
whatever the outcome
Without regret
Perhaps even
without reward

Wonder

I'm trying to catch a star
that just won't fall
Every day I wait
in search of my mission
I wait for a glimpse
of something I may not even recognize
Something I may touch
without feeling a thing
I'm waiting for a response
that speaks without
uttering any words
Searching for an answer
that yells at me in silence
and all I can see
are the movements
of the mouth
I'm trying to reach for something
that may never exist
A star that may always remain
Too high up in the sky
Too far out of reach

Clothed Eye

Your eyes see
what mine fail to acknowledge
not by choice
but by an ignorance
ingrained within
For the first time
with a new sight
I am seeing
all that I have been blind towards
Or perhaps
all that I have shunned
for the sake of my own sanity
for the purpose of my own defense
What I choose to ignore
can have no harm
because I cannot properly see
what I am looking at
The disconnection of sight
from heart and mind
does not alter
the reality of the way things are
Nor does it erase
the actuality of what is
It only glides over the surface
hoping to get a glimpse
of what lies ahead
Waiting to meet the hope
that could possibly arrive

Too Quiet

A long period of silence
enables me to forget
but only temporarily
Then the silence no longer
feels like an absence
but simply a stillness
that is calm and familiar
It is easier to adjust to
All else is drowned out
and I find myself underwater
without having to hold my breath
Everything else is in motion
but the silence remains
As I struggle to keep still

Part II

Fraser Island

I still remember that night so vividly
The pool tables, the cues
playing match after match
Winning or losing I cannot recall
but your eyes and your smile
are engraved in my mind
The glances from afar
The stares you gave so willingly
The ones that told me
that I was the most beautiful girl
you had ever laid eyes on
The night turned into fun banter
the playfulness
the chemistry undeniable
By the end of the evening
when you pulled me towards you
and wrapped your arms around me
I was at a loss for words
It was one of those feelings you never forget
It was just you, just me, just us
People thought we had been together for ages
Little did they know that we had only just met
in a country foreign to both of us
I still don't know what to call what we had;
a romance, a fling, a fleeting relationship?
But I do know that it was something special
It was also something we both knew would end
when it was time to go our separate ways
We truly lived in the moment
Were so carefree

and took advantage of our time together
I don't ever think what if we had more time
or what if we lived in the same city
I knew our paths would never cross again
But what I do think is that you were one of
the best memories from abroad
and a Matt I'll never forget

Firecracker

When he sees her
he wants to hold her
when she speaks
he wants to kiss her
when she's not around
he can't stop thinking about her
She was like a blazing fire
that was impossible to extinguish
Whenever he went to touch her
she would burn him and it would hurt
The scars left on him
are a constant reminder
of all the pain he endured
Still, despite all the pain
He yearns to be a part of that fire

Wales

You didn't captivate me
when I first saw you
In fact, you threw me off
and made me question my sanity
as I stepped on your soil
It was like a journey back in time
only to be a reality for the present day
One that I wasn't sure I would be able to adapt to
Your small-town feel was too archaic for me
The city girl in me couldn't fathom how I would cope
I saw more sheep than human beings on my commute
More bottles of freshly milked dairy than actual cartons
It was a bit of a culture shock
But as the days progressed
I learned to appreciate you
and my love for you began to expand
My heart began to well up at your beauty
Your scenery
Your speech
Your slang
Your culture
Your hidden talents
I was so taken by you and your understated beauty
You were a hidden gem no doubt
I had no idea how you would eventually take my breath away
Unbeknownst to me
you stole my heart
I realized it when we said goodbye
I knew I would yearn for you

but not in the way I have recently
A longing so strong
I want more than anything to reunite with you
I love you enough to sport a top with your name on it
which says a lot
Being with you those few years
taught me that beneath the city girl exterior
I'm all country deep down
Wales, you will always have a piece of my heart

Sorry to Say Goodbye

Been thinking about you lately
after all this time
I'm not sure why
Not particularly because I miss you
but you cross my mind
every now and then
Looking back I think I was more attracted
to the way you cherished me
and the way
you couldn't take your eyes off me
The weight of them stalking my every move
Your stare
I still feel the intensity
in your beautiful crystal clear blue eyes
whenever they met mine
I never had to question whether or not
I was the object of your affection
I knew I was

It was the love letters you sent me in the mail
everyday for a month that drew me in
I still have them tucked away somewhere
But it was the final letter from you
that made me realize
the extremity of your feelings
The one written from your cut flesh
It was such a grand act
The sincerity and genuineness of that gesture
touched me in a way I never expressed to you
That is my one regret

I wish you knew how loudly it spoke to me
Even though I could not reciprocate your feelings
you were so generous with yours
Emotionally, you were so open and so willing
to be all that you could be for me
I shut you out but wanted to let you in
I thought it could've been a possibility
but then it all shifted
like we were standing on uneven pavement
I woke up one day
and whatever feelings I had for you dissipated
without warning
without a fade
They just disappeared
I almost wished they would've somehow come back
but they didn't and I knew they wouldn't

I remember that day so clearly
I was left standing there in front of you
in that dark hallway with your eyes glistening
from the way your heart was breaking
You held my hands in yours
squeezing them so tightly
Pleading with me to give us a chance
To allow it to proceed
regardless of the state of my heart
once again declaring your love for me
I didn't know what to say
but I knew it was time for me to leave
I can barely remember the goodbye
but the finality of the situation was certain

I never wanted to hurt you
I hope you understand that at some point
I did wish that you were it too

Kampala

The wells form in my eyes
I remember your faces
I recall the moments
awakened by laughter
singing in my ears
I remember the waves;
hello and goodbye
The same gesture
that had two different meanings
The excitement
as I became visible in your sight
Clinging to my legs
Holding my hand
Touching my hair
Anything for a chance
to engage in some sort of affection
The time comes
to say goodbye
but this time
it will not be returned
with a hello anytime soon
I try to be strong
but can no longer pretend
it doesn't hurt
The tears are endless
I cannot hide the pain
All your faces watch mine
in wonder
Too young to understand

Abandoned

So small
So tough
you wouldn't let anyone near
Every touch you rejected
with a push
a shove
a grunt of disapproval
So persistent on fighting
So resistant to touch
You only wanted the attention
you never received
when you needed it most
and it wasn't available
Now it would have to be earned
with a guarantee
So small
So strong willed
Yet for a reason
Too torn
Too broken
Too hurt
But too small
far too small
and too young
to be so aware

Jesse

My heart is won over
by the glaze in your eyes
So transparent
So hollow
Eyes so blank
I hear the cries
echoing in my ear
But no tears fall
I can see your face
longing to be seen
I can feel your heart
waiting to be acknowledged
I can hear it crying out
I cannot turn my eyes away
It's a numbing pain
residing in you
and me
I'm torn
My heart is broken
and half of it belongs to you

Part III

Your Stare

I didn't like you
the moment I met you
But found that the more
you came into view
the more I enjoyed
your presence
There was something about your eyes
Your hawk-like stare
that would not give way
You captured my attention
but I didn't realize how much
until we said our final goodbye
The days that followed
could not stop you
from entering my mind
It was the first time
in a long time
that someone was able
to get to me
in a way I could not verbalize
From what I got to know of you
in a span of three days
made me wish
there were just a few more days
to get to know you better

Thinking of You

A grip so tight
This hold that won't let go
You march through my mind
stomping around the edges of my heart
The pound that coincides
with the beat of it
The sound penetrates
in my mind
and reminds me
only of the ache
that is felt within
from the separation
that cannot be bridged
My feelings are long overdue
But they do not expire
Instead, they endure
continuously
Without my consent

Starved

A smile so charming
you'd never suspect
the loneliness that is hidden
behind its assurance
The emptiness that resides
so permanently
within the corners of your heart
The search for meaning
that never rests
Intimacy sought after
to heal the ache
that exists within
A temporary fix
that only contributes
to the awareness of the void
that does not leave you alone
Your hunger and yearning
for the kind of affection
that is forbidden for a time
for all the right reasons
Yet for all the wrong reasons
you pursue it
you embrace it
you stare it right in the eye
and indulge in the solution
to the hollowness inside
But still
it is a constant reminder

of your famished soul
that will always be
less than partially full

Memories

You just stood there
looking at me
waiting for me to answer
a question you were too afraid to ask
Then you realized
it was the first time
your grip was too weak
You were trying to hang on to something
that was never yours to begin with
Now you're sorry
and I am too
I thought there would be more to you
More essence
More depth
But all I discovered was a shallowness
that would never escalate to its full potential
A setback worth recognizing
worth accepting
worth admitting
When the anticipation ceased from leading
I knew it was the memory I adored
Not you

Fallen

The feelings that lead me
down this path of speculation
have been erased
The emotions that coincided
with the thoughts
have been deflated by a truth
that was deceived by you
and by my own wishful heart
You were created in my memory
as someone I wanted you to be
But you turned out
to be quite the contrary
How could it be
that in such a short time
you became so translucent
in my eyes
My view of you has changed
You've fallen from the tip
of the highest mountain
to the bottomless ocean
and you continue to fall
into the depths of uncertainty

The Journey

When I looked into your eyes
I found I knew my way around
It was a familiar place
somewhere I had been before
You were right in front of me
just the way I had imagined it to be
But somehow I found the desire
of reverting back to my dream
more alluring
The impression of you in my mind
now so easy to release
But the memory of the time
it took to reach that moment
will always remain
a stimulating voyage
You consumed portions of my mind
My thoughts dedicated
to the memory of you
and our first meeting
I offered you a little piece of my heart
without knowing you could never break it
that you would never
come close

Your Gaze

When you look at me
your eyes devour me
All my thoughts escape me
I'm in a different world
When you look at me
you reveal more than I can contain
It's in your eyes
The way they stalk mine
I'm instantly hypnotized
When you look at me
I am completely lost
and I never want to be found

Hollow Eyes

I watched you as you gazed at me
It was the familiar eyes
but the effect was not the same
My eyes now reciprocate hollowness
that remains empty
Now in your company
the feeling no longer
triggers a curiosity
that hunts for a resolution
But instead meets a satisfaction
of knowing there no longer
remains a bout of anticipation
beneath the exposed
The genuineness of my emotions
cannot be denied
but only for the time they suffered
the long sought after explanation
Only to be deceived
by the fantasy of the heart's desire
To have you be
someone you are far from reaching
My feelings have now been terminated
demolished by the reality of truth
What began as a pleasant memory
was gradually washed away
and all that is left
are the stains in your character
that will never fade

The End

By the time the demise
of my relationship came to fruition
I was fine
ready to move forward
I had grieved its end
for the duration leading up to the split
Mourning while I was still in it
Knowing what would soon transpire
I was physically present
but emotionally checked out
Counting down the days
until I could muster up the courage
to break free from the cage
I placed myself in

I knew something wasn't right
from the beginning
But I stayed in it anyway
So many regrets
I telepathically told myself I would have them
Yet I chose to ignore it
Moving ahead was the easy part
The internal healing
that was needed in the aftermath
was an extensive and painful
but necessary journey
One I had waited too long to address

The ending signified a new beginning
to something I needed my whole life
I just didn't realize it

until I had opened up to receive
the one thing my heart needed most
And it changed everything
The epiphany I realized
much too late for my liking
I thought I knew what love was
I realized I had never come close
The demise of my relationship
was the greatest thing to happen to me
It not only signified the conclusion of the past
But also the birthing of something new

Regret

I watched you revolve your life
around something that offered you a slow death
I saw the way it altered your personality
made you happy and verbal
then depressed and mute
It brought out the extrovert in you
that went into hiding when you were sober
You were equally charming without it
but somehow felt you needed the liquid courage
What I once found endearing
turned me right off
I struggled with hiding the contempt I felt
watching you act like a fool
You quickly went from man to boy to infant
Shrinking in masculinity with every sip
I watched how it had such a grip on you
Choked every bit of motivation
and zest for life right out of you

You chose to make the bottle your priority
Every time it called you went running
Pleas for you to stop kept falling on deaf ears
The interventions met with empty assurances to stop
Only for the cycle to begin again
The viciousness and repetitiousness of it
made my head spin
I understand now how it ruins relationships

From the beginning I had a sense
that what I was about to embark on

would have devastating results
I was right
I didn't need the confirmation
but I waited for it
The longer I stayed with you
made me become someone I no longer recognized
Someone I started to despise
Someone I didn't want to be
I put myself through the emotional and mental turmoil
It was my own fault
But it made unloving you easier
Now I'm gone and I feel lighter
almost like I could float
Leaving you was the best decision for both of us
I finally feel the freedom I've been longing for
I don't regret the entire journey
Just parts of it
Actually, maybe most of it

My Name

You call out my name
but it doesn't sound like it belongs to me
I hear you yelling at the top of your lungs
but the tone of your voice
does not reach me the way you want it to
Flowing from your lips
is the desire to be heard
but my ears turn away
tired of listening to the sound of my name
coming from your mouth
My name
It rings
It echoes
In your eyes I see you pleading for me to respond
but I cannot do it
For a brief second
I wish my name was not mine

The One From Boston

If only you knew how much
I still wonder about you
Although our encounter was brief
you left a lasting impression
that hasn't worn off
Reminiscing about that day
brings a smile to my face
and whenever I'm at the airport
I'm reminded of that time
I was waiting for the bus to arrive
and took a pause from my phone
Briefly looked up and around
and there you were
standing right behind me the whole time
Tall, dark hair and incredibly good looking

As we boarded the bus
you came and planted yourself right next to me
And our dialogue began
with where we were from
to where we were going
The conversation flowed as laughter ensued
We spent a vast amount of time
talking about wineries;
Napa and the Okanagan
Probably because it was where you were headed
for your annual trip with your sibling
You made comparisons
between the names of the wineries

and what they sounded like in a hushed tone
Your use of the word touché made me laugh

Time soared and
the next thing I knew
we were at our destination
It was one of the few times
I would've welcomed a delay
You thoughtfully lifted my suitcase for me
then we said a hurried goodbye
I turned right, you proceeded left
and we were swallowed up by the crowd
It was unusually hectic and congested
We were so immersed in our conversation
I forgot to ask for your name
There were so many other things
I learned about you
But I never found out your name

Although I know I will never see you again
I feel blessed to have experienced
that fleeting encounter
You will always be known as that guy from Boston
And one day when someone asks if I've ever been there
I'll reply, no, but I once met a guy from there
who made my heart flutter
But never knew
Because I couldn't find him
so I could tell him

Where Were You?

I see you cry the tears
that don't fall
I hear the thoughts
you cannot articulate
I watch the movements you make
without any motions
You think you've out cried yourself
but the pain
embedded in your memory
seared on your heart
still cries in your soul
The comfort and healing
taking far too long to arrive

You took things into your own hands
attacking those who should have been there to help you
With clenched fists
and furrowed brows
you yell and scream
Where were you?
Where were you?!

Part IV

Beauty

True beauty
is breathtaking
It stuns
It captivates
It intrigues
It revitalizes
It shines from the inside out
It's more than just a word
that defines an indescribable awe
you feel towards something
It captures more than
what you see outwardly
True beauty isn't fleeting
It doesn't age
It's constant
Like God's love
It never fades
It coexists with identity
in the one who created you
It's contagious
It doesn't warn you
or announce itself
It doesn't need to
It knows who you are

My Reason

You said follow me
so I took a step forward
only to turn around
and sprint away
Slowly then the marathon began
I was on an endless race
to find the very thing
I was running from
I thought I lost something
that was already stored away
in my heart
It was never missing
It simply needed to resurface
in its own time
You showed up so quietly
but not suddenly
Your presence overpowering
but not invading
Like a true gentleman
you tenderly pounded on my door
then waited and waited
Awakening me to my senses
in such a way
you didn't need to say a word
Your presence alone
was enough for me to feel
all you had been waiting to tell me
throughout the years
If only I had opened my heart to hear

As you began to speak
I stood and listened
then sat and cried
I fell on my face
and sobbed
until my tears ran dry
Heaving
I felt my heart breaking
like shattered glass
I gathered up the pieces
and held them in my hands
and on my knees before you
I gave you what was already yours
Ever so graciously
you mended my heart back together
with no evidence of the scars
It now beats differently
because it has been
connected to yours
You've given me the greatest gift
One I never deserved
My life now has new meaning
It's richer
My heart is full
My purpose is clear
You, are my reason for being

Surrender

Buried far too deep within your soul
is that tiny space
left untouched
Guarded so carefully by your heart
Too afraid to let anything slip through
It's there I want to reside
because once I'm inhabited there
the rest of you lives and breathes
Without abandon
You come alive
You're awakened
with a sense of completeness
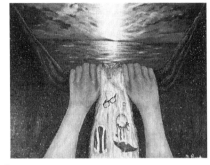
An indescribable feeling of contentment
in knowing who you are through me
Mere glimpses of your tiny space will not suffice
The peeks you give me bring no satisfaction.
Allow me to engulf it with my being
And you will experience
the fullness of yourself
And what it really means to live

Freedom

You came and awakened parts of me
I didn't know existed
Feelings I never knew I could feel
Emotions I never knew I could express
Like a thief you stole the one thing
I kept caged and locked up
My heart
You hijacked then released it
allowing it the freedom to be itself
without the barriers
You've enabled it to open up
and become the fullness of
what it is
But most importantly who it should be
It's in this love
I'm unable to adequately articulate
because words fail me
But I would fail you in my description
of what I now feel
because you are inexpressible
You are tangible only in my heart and soul
Without you I am unable to find my way
You are my greatest treasure
yet you are the one
who found and rescued me from destruction
and have enriched my life in the process
My heart
Now belonging to you
Dances with your every breath

Bursting with joy
and coming alive more each day
It's in your love my heart lives and breathes
It is with you
I want to reside for eternity

Trust

I'm choosing to trust
I keep choosing
because it's the only hope I have
It's the only certainty I hang on to with dear life
Your promises are what keep me going
Your words of affirmation
of a love that'll never abandon me
or make me have to earn it
The purity of your goodness
is what allows me to keep trusting you
in the midst of the unsteadiness
Your reassurance in having heard my cries
Your fatherly love that unconditionally consoles me
especially when I start to doubt
when I begin to lose the hope I should have
In the waiting is a hard place to be
yet I continue to cling to your words
To your heart for me
To your goodness
To your promises
that will be fulfilled in your timing
and understanding why it's not happening in my own
You see the bigger picture
of what I only see mere fractions of
Pieces that barely make sense to my small mind
This is why I keep choosing
to keep trusting
It's your faithfulness
that restores my moments of distrust
and continues to remind me
How faithful you are

Where you go, I go

I sit here in the quiet
numbed by the stillness
wanting so badly
to tangibly feel you near
Close enough for me to rest
my head on your chest
You're here
yet I'm having trouble
articulating your proximity to me
I think if I could just measure it
I'll know just how close you are
I keep grasping at the air around me
wanting to grab a hold of something
that I can't physically touch
I'm asking the same questions
making the same statements
wishing, waiting, wanting, wailing
for a response I can understand
decipher in my own mind

The silence is deafening
unbearable at times
I know, I know it's the timing
and it's in the waiting
that stretches the trust
I feel is going to break
each time another day passes
I'm learning patience
more of it with each passing day
I'm operating based on time

and have to remind myself
you define it differently than I do
I'm trying hard
to get on the same page as you
to have my heart beat in tune with yours
To allow you to lead without having to know
where you're taking me
I've come to a standstill and I'm feeling cocooned
trying to slowly break free again
My time of rest is coming to an end
and I'm pushing through
with the edge of my wing
Eagerly anticipating breaking out
and flying high in the unknown
not wanting to do it prematurely

The silence
still echoing in my ears
I'm wondering how to keep a thought stagnant
without it vibrating all around me
Despite that
I can only keep trudging forward
sprinting up the mountain
when I would so much rather slide down it
I know clarity will come
with every step united with yours
Sometimes you move too quickly
I can barely keep up
Other times I'm running far ahead of you
begging you to catch up
The key is alignment
I've found it
So in this silence
I choose to continuously

search, seek and rely on you
To watch for the movements of your mouth
and listen to the nudges that steer me
straight into your shadow
Wherever you lead
I will follow

Always You

It's you
It's always been you
I was just unaware at the time
You loved me first
throughout the years
and I barely caught a glimpse
Until now
I feel it
I hear it
My heart sees it
and I've come undone
My insides overflow
with desire and a hunger to love you
just as much as you love me
I'm here now
fully surrendered to your will
waiting for you to reveal more
I long to go deeper
to know your heart
to see things
and to love the way you do
I feel you encapsulate me
and I melt in your arms
while I wonder how it is possible
to feel so cherished
You alone make up for everything
I never had in my life
And you are all I will ever need
and more
It's you

It's always been you
My one true love
The absolute love of my life
I never knew what it meant
until now
It's you

Thanks so much for journeying with me through this book

Manufactured by Amazon.ca
Bolton, ON

22345100R00059